מַעֲרָכָה ArtScroll Youth Series ®

"Just a

Published by

Mesorah Publications, ltd

in conjunction with

ArtScroll / ירושלים בע"מ אטסקרול
Jerusalem, ltd.

Week to Go"

ONE BOY'S PESACH PREPARATIONS IN JERUSALEM'S OLD CITY

by Yeshara Gold

Photographs by Yaacov Harlap
and Yeshara Gold

My deep appreciation
To Shoshana Lepon for her encouragement and wise counsel,
To Robert Mann for his continued support
of Jewish educational projects,
And to Raphael who made "Just a Week To Go"
a pleasure to produce.

This book is gratefully dedicated to
Shalom
May we all find merit in Hashem's eyes.

Yeshara Gold

FIRST EDITION
First Impression ... March 1987
Second Impression ... February 2001

Published and Distributed by
MESORAH PUBLICATIONS, LTD.
4401 Second Avenue / Brooklyn, N.Y 11232

Distributed in Europe by
LEHMANNS
Unit E, Viking Industrial Park
Rolling Mill Road
Jarrow, Tyne & Wear, NE32 3DP
England

Distributed in Australia and New Zealand
by **GOLDS WORLD OF JUDAICA**
3-13 William Street
Balaclava, Melbourne 3183
Victoria Australia

Distributed in Israel by
SIFRIATI / A. GITLER
6 Hayarkon Street
Bnei Brak 51127

Distributed in South Africa by
KOLLEL BOOKSHOP
Shop 8A Norwood Hypermarket
Norwood 2196, Johannesburg, South Africa

ARTSCROLL SERIES®
"JUST A WEEK TO GO"
© Copyright 2000, by MESORAH PUBLICATIONS, Ltd.
4401 Second Avenue / Brooklyn, N.Y. 11232 / (718) 921-9000 / www.artscroll.com

ISBN:
0-89906-802-2 (hard cover)
0-89906-803-0 (paperback)

Typography by CompuScribe at ArtScroll Studios, Ltd.
Printed in the United States of America by Edison Printing Corp.
Bound by Sefercraft, Quality Bookbinders, Ltd., Brooklyn N.Y. 11232

"Just a Week to Go"

Glossary

Abba	Daddy
bedikat chametz	ridding home of *chametz* before Passover
brit milah	circumcision
chagigah	an animal offering in the Holy Temple in Jerusalem
chametz	grain products not in accord with Passover requirements
cheder	elementary school
chessed	acts of kindness
Eliyahu Hanavi	Elijah the Prophet
Eretz Yisrael	Land of Israel
hagalat keilim	"koshering" utensils for Passover use
Haggadah	text of the *seder* service
Hashem	"the Name," a reference to G-d
Imma	Mommy
keilim	utensils, such as pots, pans, silverware, cutlery
kollel	community of married yeshivah students
Kotel	Western Wall
Mah nishtanah ...	The Four Questions asked at the *seder*
maot chitim	charity given to the needy before Passover
matzah [pl. matzot]	unleavened bread
mitzvah [pl. mitzvot]	a commandment of G-d; generally, a good deed
Moshe Rabbeinu	Moses our Teacher
Pesach	Passover
Rosh Yeshivah	dean of a *yeshivah*
seder	retelling of the Exodus with the accompanying rituals and feast
sefer [pl. sefarim]	books
shemurah matzah	matzah prepared from wheat that was guarded against moisture from the moment it was cut
siyum	completion of the study of a volume of the Talmud
Torah	Scriptures
Yerushalayim	Jerusalem
yeshivah	school of Torah study
yetzer hara	the Evil Inclination

"**M**ah nishtanah halailah hazeh ..." It's the last day of cheder before Pesach vacation and all my friends are practicing the four questions. At our seder we must ask them clearly — "Why is this night different from all other nights?"

We all want to be like the wise son in the Haggadah. The son who knows how to ask.

My name is Raffi and I live in the Old City of *Yerushalayim*. I'm in a hurry to get home because I want to start getting ready for *Pesach*. It is still a week away but there is so much to do. In just one week we

will all be going out of Egypt. The *Haggadah* is not just a story about an adventure that happened long ago. Every year at the *seder*, we should feel that we are going free again. That's why I'm so excited about *Pesach*. On *Pesach* night we will all become free. There's just a week to go!

❧　　❧　　❧

"*Imma*, I'm home. Where should I start cleaning for *Pesach*?"

"I'm glad you have so much energy. After your snack you can begin cleaning out the *chametz* in your books and toys."

Chametz is flour that got wet and had time to grow higher. The Jews rushed out of Egypt in such a hurry that they didn't even have time to let their dough rise. They made flat bread called *matzah*. To remember this, *Hashem* told us to eat only *matzah* during the week of *Pesach*. We're not even allowed to keep *chametz* in our homes!

"*Chametz, Chametz,* where are you?" laughs my little sister Ellyana. She is only two years old and doesn't understand what a serious job it is to get rid of *chametz*.

"*Chametz,* I found you!" Ellyana giggles.

Well, the *Torah* does say that we should do the work of *Hashem* with joy, so I guess it's okay for Elly to find fun along with the *chametz*.

❀   ❀   ❀

I take out my *sefarim* one by one and check every page. *Abba* showed me how to blow on each page to get out the tiniest crumbs.

Just as *chametz* is puffed up flour, the *yetzer hara* tries to puff us up with pride. My teacher Rebbe Moshe taught us that we should think of getting rid of our *yetzer hara* along with the *chametz*.

Abba wrote the words *matzah* (מצה) and *chametz* (חמץ) on my chalk board. The letters of the two words are the same except for the ה and the ח. If the line in the ה were a little bit longer it would turn into a ח, and the letters of the word *matzah* would become the letters of *chametz*. In the same way the bakers in the *matzah* factory must be very careful not to take even a bit longer so that their *matzah* does not turn into *chametz*.

For Pesach, *Abba* makes raisin wine. He buys grapes and dries them in the sun to make his own juicy raisins. Then he soaks the raisins in water for three days. There is enough sweet wine for all our *seder guests,* and for the *Rosh Yeshivah* of our *kollel,* too.

At last, our kitchen is ready for *Pesach*. It was a big job ... everything was scrubbed and koshered.

Some pots, pans and silverware can be made kosher for Pesach by boiling them. This is called *hagalat keilim*. I like to watch when the men dunk the *keilim* into huge vats of boiling water. I don't get too close because it's a little bit scary and very dangerous!

I get to go with *Abba* to the *matzah* factory.

The *matzah* we eat on *Pesach* is very special. It is called *shemurah matzah* because it is always guarded to make sure it does not get wet and become *chametz*. We start guarding it from the minute the wheat is cut in the field.

The bakers' hands seem to fly as they roll out the dough. The *matzah* must be completed without wasting time. If it takes too long, the dough might become *chametz*. When I see the bakers in such a hurry I think of how fast we had to leave Egypt. *Hashem* knew exactly when it was time for us to go

free. When it was time to go, we could not wait an extra second.

The baker taught me how to make little holes in the dough with a special roller so that the *matzah* would get baked through and through.

"*L'shem matzot mitzvah*," echoes in the factory, "for the *mitzvah* of *matzah*". The bakers say this every

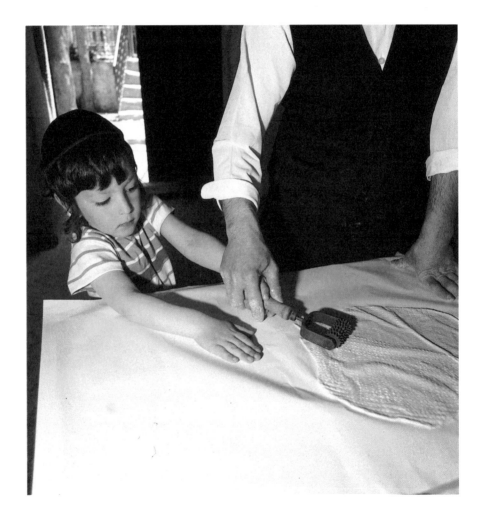

few minutes, keeping *Hashem's* commandment in mind as they make each *matzah.*

❊ ❊ ❊

The *matzah* bakers told us how this oven stays hot enough to bake *matzot.* They burn olive wood in the oven for three days before it is hot enough to bake the first *matzah.* Sand and salt under the stones help keep in the heat.

❊ ❊ ❊

The *matzah* dough is carried to the oven on a pole and placed on hot bricks.

Hashem did a great *chessed* by taking us out of Egypt. On *Pesach* we try to do *chessed* also. We give *maot chitim,* money for poor people to buy *matzah* and wine.

I like to help pack and give out the kosher-for-*Pesach* food at Ezrat Avot, a Yemenite community center. *Abba* says that when every Jew sits down to his *seder* he should know that other Jews have what they need, too.

Imma and I go to the Machaneh Yehudah market to shop for the *seder*. We need to buy six things for the *seder* plate … *karpas, maror, chazeret, charoset,* shankbone, and an **egg**.

Karpas is usually celery, parsley, or potatoes. My rebbe said that we dip the *karpas* into salt water before we eat it. The salt reminds us that we were once slaves, and dipping reminds us that we are now free.

Abba grates up horseradish for *maror*. It makes us cry and reminds us how bitter our lives were in Egypt.

Chazeret is another type of bitter vegetable. Abba uses romaine lettuce. It is sweet at first but leaves a bad taste in the mouth. That is like our time in Egypt. At first we were welcomed and given the best land. But soon, the Egyptians forgot all that Joseph had done for them. They treated us badly.

Charoset looks like the bricks we made to build Pharaoh's cities. I like the *charoset* that *Imma* makes with wine, nuts, cinnamon, and apples. The red wine reminds us of the blood of the little boys that Pharaoh killed. The Jewish fathers were so sad that they didn't want to have any more children. But the Jewish mothers gave them new hope. They pointed to the apple tree and said, "Just as the apple tree first brings fruit and then grows the leaves to guard it, so should we have children now and afterwards *Hashem* will guard them."

The butcher's wife gives me a shankbone. We put it on the *seder* plate to remind us of the *Korban Pesach*. The Egyptians made the lamb their idol. To show that Jews don't believe in idols, *Hashem* commanded them to slaughter a lamb and sprinkle its blood on their doorposts. We were not afraid to listen to *Hashem*, even though we knew that our Egyptian masters would get angry. This sign on the doorposts saved the Jewish firstborn sons when all the Egyptian firstborn died that night.

The last thing we have to buy for the *seder* plate is an egg. The hard boiled egg takes the place of the *chagigah* sacrifice. *Imma* told me that the egg is the only food that gets harder as it boils. All other foods get soft and fall apart, but the egg gets tougher and tougher. That is like the Jewish people. Other nations have fallen apart, but the Jews always grow stronger.

A few days before *Pesach*, *Abba* and I go to see Rabbi Getz, the *Rav* of the *Kotel*. Since we are not allowed to own *chametz*, we must sell our *chametz* to a non-Jew. Selling *chametz* is complicated, so we ask Rabbi Getz to do it for us. We meet with him in the tunnel alongside the *Kotel*.

Look, it's raining! Here in *Eretz Yisrael*, we pray for rain from *Sukkot* until *Pesach*. This will probably be the last rain of the year, just in time to wash the *chametz* away. *Hashem* is cleaning for *Pesach,* too!

"*Abba*, here is the candle, feather and wooden spoon. We're ready to start *bedikat chametz*."

We've been working for weeks. We've cleaned out the *chametz* room by room. Now, the night before *Pesach*, it is time for the last search. I hide ten pieces of *chametz* for *Abba* to find. With our candle we search the darkened house and sweep the *chametz* with the feather onto the wooden spoon. These last bits of *chametz* will be burned in the morning.

"*Abba*, I can smell the fires outside. When are we going to burn our *chametz*?"

Fires all over *Yerushalayim* burn the last bits of *chametz*. I meet my friends and their families outside. Everyone looks happy to be rid of their *chametz* for this year.

[28]　"Just a Week to Go"

"Come on, my *bechor*. It's time to go."

The firstborn son is called a *bechor*. *Hashem* struck the Egyptians with ten plagues. The last plague was the killing of their firstborn sons. But *Hashem* saved the sons of the Jews. For this reason firstborn sons thank *Hashem* by fasting on the day before *Pesach*. My *Abba* is a *bechor* and I am one too!

This fast can be broken at a meal served to celebrate a *mitzvah,* such as a *brit milah* or the completion of a volume of the Talmud. *Abba* and I are going to the Ramban *Shul* for a *siyum*.

Imma and Elly have already started to set the table. In long ago times, noblemen relaxed on couches when they ate. On *Pesach* we became *Hashem's* chosen people. That's why we lean on our left sides during the *seder*. *Imma* puts pillows and quilts all around, so we'll be cozy and comfortable. *Pesach* surely is different from all other nights!

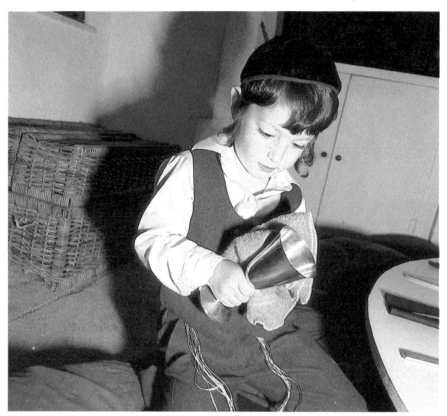

I polish *Eliyahu's* cup over and over. We drink four cups of wine at the *seder,* but a fifth cup is put on the table just for *Eliyahu Hanavi.* I get to open the door to let him in. I've never seen him, but I know he comes to everyone's *seder* and takes a sip. I want our cup to really shine in honor of *Eliyahu.*

I carry three *matzot* to the table and put them gently under their cover. They must be whole and unbroken for the *seder.*

Well, everything is ready. I can't believe that we did so much in one week. And I even found time to practice "*Mah nishtanah...*"

The *Torah* says "You shall tell your child ..." That is why *Abba* tells the story of our going out of Egypt. When *Abba* was a little boy his father used to tell him, and his grandfather used to tell his father, all the way back to the time of *Moshe Rabbeinu.*

When I become an *Abba,* I'll tell the story to my children, too! I'll tell them "why this night is different from all other nights." I'll tell them that on this night all Jews go out to freedom!

לשנה הבאה בירושלים!

Next year may all Jews celebrate Pesach in Yerushalayim!